John Clifford

Social Worship

An everlasting necessity

John Clifford

Social Worship
An everlasting necessity

ISBN/EAN: 9783741176302

Manufactured in Europe, USA, Canada, Australia, Japa

Cover: Foto ©Andreas Hilbeck / pixelio.de

Manufactured and distributed by brebook publishing software (www.brebook.com)

John Clifford

Social Worship

SMALL BOOKS ON GREAT SUBJECTS.

Pott 8vo, in Buckram Cloth, price 1s. 6d. each.

1. **Words by the Wayside.** By GEORGE MATHESON, M.A., D.D., F.R.S.E. [*Second Edition.*
2. **Faith the beginning, Self-surrender the fulfilment, of the Spiritual Life.** By JAMES MARTINEAU, D.D., D.C.L. [*Second Edition.*
3. **Reconsiderations and Reinforcements.** By J. M. WHITON, Ph.D., Author of "Beyond the Shadow," &c.
4. **Mischievous Goodness, AND OTHER PAPERS.** By CHARLES A. BERRY, D.D.
5. **The Jealousy of God, AND OTHER PAPERS.** By JOHN PULSFORD, D.D., Author of "Quiet Hours," &c.
6. **How to Become like Christ, AND OTHER PAPERS.** By MARCUS DODS, D.D. [*Second Edition.*
7. **Character through Inspiration, AND OTHER PAPERS.** By T. T. MUNGER, D.D., Author of "The Freedom of Faith," &c.
8. **Chapters in the Christian Life.** By the Ven. W. M. SINCLAIR, D.D., Archdeacon of London.
9. **The Angels of God, AND OTHER PAPERS.** By JOHN HUNTER, D.D.
10. **The Conquered World, AND OTHER PAPERS.** By R. F. HORTON, M.A., D.D.
11. **The Making of an Apostle.** By R. J. CAMPBELL, of Brighton.
12. **The Ship of the Soul, AND OTHER PAPERS.** By STOPFORD A. BROOKE, M.A.
13. **The Way of Life.** By H. ARNOLD THOMAS, M.A.
14. **Social Worship: an Everlasting Necessity.** By J. CLIFFORD, M.A., D.D.

Small Books on Great Subjects.—XIV.

SOCIAL WORSHIP
 By JOHN CLIFFORD, M.A., D.D.

SOCIAL WORSHIP:
An Everlasting Necessity

By John Clifford, M.A., D.D.
Author of "Christian Certainties,"
"Typical Christian Leaders," &c.

LONDON: JAMES CLARKE & CO.
13 & 14, Fleet Street. 1899.

First Edition, June, 1899.

Contents.

	PAGE
Social Worship: An Everlasting Necessity	1
God the Home of the Soul	26
How Paul thought of the Incarnation	36
Jesus Praying	48
The Church of the Ages	70
Lives that Make Music	84
Strength for Tired Men	100
The Idea of Eternity in the Bible and Human Life	127
The Better Resurrection	137

Social Worship: An Everlasting Necessity.

"We have thought of Thy lovingkindness, O God, in the midst of Thy temple."
—PSALM XLVIII. 9.

SIXTY years ago Emerson told the divinity students at Cambridge that "public worship had lost its grasp on the affection of the good and the fear of the bad," and "that what hold it had on men generally was gone or going." At last, it seemed, men had found out the vanity of the hoary habit inherited from the fathers of our race. They saw it lacked soul and light, reality and humanness, moral healing and spiritual uplifting. Good men felt it a duty to avoid it, and many of those who still clung to the ancient custom were moved, not by joy and gratitude, but by a withered hope, destined to be cut off.

Echoes of such a reading of passing moods in the life of man reach us to-day concerning ourselves and our habits of thought and action. Social worship, it is said, is losing its central place in the experience of troubled men; the persecuted and perplexed no longer soothe their grief and feed their faith by recalling the visions of the Eternal; visions that once filled their souls as they thought and prayed in the temples of God. "Literary" men, writers of books, and editors of newspapers know not our churches except for "copy"; "working men" scorn them, and the ordinances of worship are so materialised that one of our critics tells us we must "abolish our churches and make a bonfire of our Prayer-books to discover who the really religious are." The Saxon of to-day is altogether incapable of the holy pride and devout exultation which filled the Jew as he sang:

We think of Thy lovingkindness, O God,
In the midst of Thy temple.
As is Thy name, O God,
So is Thy praise unto the ends of the
 earth:
Thy right hand is full of righteousness.

And then, fired by the impressive vision of the beloved building, thinking of the service it will render to posterity, he cried:

Walk about Zion, and go round about
 her:
Tell the towers thereof.
Mark ye well her bulwarks,
Consider her palaces;
That ye may tell it to the generation
 following.
For this God is our God for ever and
 ever:
He will be our guide even unto death.

But we do not despond. Emerson lived to see a general quickening of interest in social worship, and was himself one of the heralds of the dawn; nay, more, one of the creators of the day, by his insistent speech concerning the eternal sacredness of man, and the universality of the divine. Spasms of despair are not the surest guides to accurate thoughts, and momentary experiences are not always the signs of permanent tendencies. Thinking men will not lift an incident into a law, with the ease that a child flings a pebble into the sea. They will look long and all around, see life steadily and see it whole, and so find a cheering gospel where others discovered no more than doleful jeremiads about growing infidelity, and see an indication of spiritual yearning, where some very pious people who read their Bibles with "devout inattention" meet with nothing but "signs of the last times." The thermometer will not be below zero in July if it is in February, and therefore we must not reason on the whole year from what we feel to-day.

Indeed! we have so often seen the mist-filled morning leading like dark steeds the world to a bright day, that when we behold its approach, our hearts are glad and assured: and in like manner when we see census-takers at their task, and hear debaters discussing the reasons why "working men" forsake worship, and listen to the seers denouncing our coldness and formalism and our excessive ritualism and deepening death, we feel that an Emerson is at the doors, rekindling (as he himself did) the smouldering and nigh-quenched fires on the altar, and cheering the fainting hearts of men with a new hope.

Let us get down to principles and plant our feet on facts, on eternal facts, and as we see truth we shall find duty if not content, and inspiration if not satisfaction.

1. *Social Worship an Everlasting Necessity.*

For social worship is one of *the everlasting necessities of men.* They seek it as the plants the sun. They *must.* They are made for it, and made by it. It is the food of the soul, and as the Eternal God is always moving to higher effects and more spiritual realms, so the growing and expanding soul-life of man will increasingly nourish itself in the temples of social worship and Christian ministry. Aristotle says, man is "a social animal." He is, and he realises himself, his best and purest self, only by entering into relations with society, with home, village, city, and nation; and he the more swiftly and surely attains to that diviner self, as he enters sympathetically and actively into relations with the purest and noblest society. For he is spirit, and has a body, and whilst his body attains its maturity by the aid of fruitful earth and shining sun, the soul only reaches perfection through the aid of truth, of righteousness and God; and therefore the circle of spiritual friends is necessary, so that he may realise his spiritual individuality, develop faith and fortitude, love and patience, meekness and self-mastery, and all the finer qualities of a Christlike manhood.

"Every vital manifestation," says Weismann, "is a reaction to stimulus"; and "animals and plants are comparable to machines so constructed that stimuli from the outer world cause them to act in the most purposeful manner for their own maintenance." Think out that biological law and it leads straight to the cry, "O come, let us worship and bow down, let us kneel before the Lord our Maker." When the leaves of the mimosa plant are touched they close; but that is not merely to amuse the visitor to Kew Gardens; it is the plant continuing the habit of its being so that it may present the smallest surface to the desolating showers that fall in tropical climes, and thus prevent its destruction. Plants do not react to light each in the same way; but according to differences in their fine molecular structure; most of them inclining to the light, whilst the climbing shoots of the ivy turn away from it. Now man is God's child, and the spiritual "constituents" of his being only develop according to their purpose, in His presence. His spiritually vital manifestations are reactions to stimulus—that stimulus being the touch of the God who made him and redeems him and renews him. The law of social worship is that man needs God, as brain and muscle need food, the eye light, and the ear sound. It is not God's need of us; though I rejoice to think that His love for us is like that of a mother for her children, and therefore He seeks and saves us; but it is our need of Him that is the ground and reason of worship. So the normal prayer of the spirit of man is, "O God, Thou art my God; early will I seek Thee. My soul thirsteth for Thee; to see Thy power and Thy glory as I have seen Thee in the sanctuary." True, "God is," as Secker, anticipating Tennyson, says, "nearer to us than we are to ourselves"; yet in these "temples," which are the dwelling-places of *circles of spiritual friends,* who with one heart and soul worship God, He draws nigh and we realise His lovingkindness, rejoice in those aspects of His character which interpret life and give light, stir conscience and evoke faith, inflame love and quicken zeal, till we find that all is charm and zest, and peace and joy. Therefore, wherever there are "temples" where worship is real and reasonable, devout and decorous, satisfying the heart without affronting the intellect, reverent and yet full of soul, and the teaching is creative of an atmosphere devoutly magnetic and quickening, and aiding the soul in realising and enjoying God, men and women will be passing through experiences which will supply the material and inspiration for the grateful recollection:—

We have thought of Thy lovingkindness, O God, in the midst of Thy temple.

Here, then, is rock. Man needs God, God needs the love of man. Man is made for God, to enjoy Him and serve Him, in the service of His family and Kingdom for ever. Man is destined to be conformed to the image of God in Christ. This is the law of worship. And therefore we gather together for the worship of the Father, with unfaltering faith, unwithered zeal, and unclouded hope.

2. *Social Worship a School for the Realisation of God.*

But it is part of the message of Israel given in this psalm—a psalm as remarkable for its lyrical beauty as for its festive joy and its impassioned love of the sanctuary—that social worship only meets the eternal needs of men when it is a school for the realisation of God, of God in His greatness as the Lord of Life, in His lovingkindness as the Redeemer of Life, in His patience and help as the Guide of Life. "We *think;*" it is a present act; we now think of Thy lovingkindness; that is, we seek to realise Thy lovingkindness, to understand it, to feel how real and all-pervasive it is, and what guarantees it gives us that we are the cherished children of a God who knows us, loves us, desires us, redeems us, and co-operates with our efforts to read the meaning of His mysterious world, welcomes us in our efforts to co-operate with Him in achieving its redemption. The "temple" is not only a house of prayer, it is also a place of meditation, of readjusted judgments, of clearer perceptions, of soothed feelings, and of hallowed reconciliations. Like living in a refulgent summer it is a luxury to breathe. Faith grows, the vision clears, love expands, and the spirit is healed and strengthened in God Himself. Righteousness is our joy. The spiritual order appears in all its beauty and sublimity and mystery. The soul is awed and gladdened, calmed and quickened; the worshipper feels that he belongs to virtue, to holiness, to God. He is not his own. Sin is hated; the smallest mixture of vanity is an offence, and life and immortality are brought to light.

Rapt into still communion which transcends
The imperfect offices of prayer and praise;

The mind is a thanksgiving to the power
Which made it. It is blessedness and love.

There the sorely-tried exile, strained by efforts to arrange the ravelled and tangled threads of life, gathers hints of the providential wisdom that rules the world and is content; there men, puzzled with the contradictions of life, and wearied with the sound of the long, low moan, as of a wintry sea, of suffering souls, find the Ariadne clue that leads to harmony and peace; there patriots, beleagured and attacked, recall the way in which God has helped their fathers and founders to pluck up courage to say, "All our enemies will surely go down before us"; and they themselves sing as soldiers who have ascended the heights of victory, achieved a giant's task, and may move forward with fearless devotion and victory, assured that "This God is our God for ever, and will be our guide even unto death."

But must we in these days betake ourselves to man-built temples to feel the touch of God, to baptize our motives in the waters of the unseen, and to gain the heights of that Pisgah where we shall see all things truly by seeing them in God? Surely not! God's sanctuaries are not geographical. One of the wise men says in the 119th Psalm, "The earth is full of Thy lovingkindness, O God: teach me Thy statutes." All life is holy. There is no secular save in souls. It is not the temple, but God Himself, who is the explication of our perplexity, the redeemer from sin, and the beginning of our new life, and, therefore, we may realise Him and His lovingkindness—oh! how sweetly!—in the stillness of the sick-room; in the prayer-meeting, where two or three sincere souls wait all alert for the whispers of the Father; in the magnificent cathedral with its subduing or thrilling music; on the top of a mountain or by the far-resounding sea. The one thing needful is to gain somehow, somewhere, the true view-point of life and its contents, where the all-interpreting and all-loving God illumines the whole scene.

Agreed. Still Israel received an eternal truth in the assurance that its social worship offered facilities and inspirations for the realising of the lovingkindness of God rarely found elsewhere. Such worship take us out of the agitations and turmoils of the world into an atmosphere of devotion created by the fellowship of God-adoring souls. It localises the divine, shuts out the intrusive world and helps us against the tyranny of the senses. We know it. I know it. You know it. Like Peter you have said, "It is good to be on the mount that transfigures life. We have dwelt in an atmosphere subtle, impalpable, but corrosive and disintegrating to our spiritual manhood, and the soul has rusted in it, as iron in the dews of night, and we have lived and moved without realising a present God, or a lofty purpose; but we have entered into His sanctuary, and, noiselessly as the sunshine, the comforts of God have reached us, and we have felt the force of His gracious attraction, the joy of His uplifting, and the sweet impulse and rapture of His love. As to a medal placed in an appropriate solution the silver flies, in invisible flakes and molecules, without any mechanical action; so to us in that spiritual atmosphere come the redeeming and renewing energies of God, and joyfully we record our testimony: "We have thought of Thy lovingkindness, O God, in the midst of Thy temple."

One of the finest passages in

Mr. Balfour's book on "The Foundations of Belief" is that in which he gives a new setting to the familiar doctrine of environment, and tells us that "the power of authority is never more subtle and effective than when it produces a psychological 'atmosphere' or 'climate' favourable to the life of certain modes of belief, unfavourable and even fatal to the life of others. Such climates may be widely diffused or the reverse. Their range may cover a generation, an epoch, a whole civilisation, or it may be narrowed down to a sect, a family, even an individual." Now, it is one of the primary duties of the Christian Society to produce such a "psychological climate," to create opportunities for men of business and for burdened women and bewildered little children to get away from the distractions and sorrows, the contradictions and confusions of life, and quietly and simply think on

God. Incessant work destroys the power of self-collectedness and of concentration. The struggle for bread and vanity shuts out eternity. The awful might of evil becomes terrifying, even to faith; but like Asaph we go into the sanctuary of God, and if we do not understand, at least we are quieted, we grow in faith, and the presence of God becomes more and more real to us, more and more all in all; the light not only of religion, but of history, of ethics, of nation and town, of home and soul. To keep out of that "psychological climate" is to invite doubt, to dwarf the stature of the soul, to weaken the grip of ideality, to give the advantage to selfishness, just as it would be fruitlessness for all the trees of the wood to keep them in an atmosphere of perpetual frost. Again and again, men have confessed to me that their neglect of social worship has led to their neglect of all worship, their cessation from effort in the Church of Christ, and the loss of any desire to do any definite work for the helping of man. You cannot grow the finest grapes and figs at the North Pole; nor can you grow the finest manhood without a climate saturated with the worship of God.

Now, it is the distinctive function of Christianity "to fulfil" the message of Israel concerning social worship by mediating in the clearest and completest way the lovingkindness of God to the souls of men. The difference in the older and newer worship is not in its object, God; or in its purpose, the realising of His tender pity and saving mercy; but in the fuller manifestation of that pity in and through the preaching of Jesus Christ. Christianity increases the service of the temple as a mediation of God in the most helpful and life-giving aspects of His character and work. It has made preaching inevitable, given it spontaneity, a perennial freshness, and quickening frankness, by supplying as its theme "Christ crucified, the power of God, the wisdom of God": God in the tenderness of His sympathy and the fulness of His love as the inexhaustible hope of sinful men. An inadequate appreciation of Christ says:

> Never yet has been broken
> The silence eternal;
> Never yet has been spoken,
> In accents supernal,
> God's thought of Himself.
>
> Still the veil is unriven
> That hides the All-Holy:
> Still no token is given
> That satisfies wholly
> The cravings of man.
>
> But, unhasting, advances
> The march of the ages:
> To truth-seekers' glances
> Unrolling the pages
> Of God's revelation.

But Jesus assures us, "He that

has seen Me has seen the Father," and the ages cry "Amen." Therefore, seeing we have such a revelation, we must speak the things we have seen and heard: for the things are mercy and peace, forgiveness of sins, the deliverance from death, the harmonising of the conflicting elements of life, the triumph over evil, and the life for evermore. The function of the Christian minister is to aid men in realising the love of God and in showing love to men, and he only succeeds in the degree in which he attains those ends. He is not a builder of theologies, though if he does not know them, he is likely to be led captive by many an ancient error in new attire, or a new falsehood in ancient garb; he is not merely a teacher of ethics, and yet if he does not aid the highest morality he misses his goal; he is not an engineer of charitable and educational societies, and yet he will lose many an opportunity of advancing the Kingdom of God if he does not handle all knowledge, stir generous emotions and elicit generous gifts; least of all is he the richly-robed performer of a florid ritual. No! he is the messenger of God as revealed in Jesus, speaking to men who have come to think on His lovingkindness, and who want to find in it the solution of their perplexities, the healing of their diseases, the food for their maintenance, the weapon for their resistance of evil, and the means of their victory over death. "To know God," says Carlyle, "the Maker, to know the Divine Laws and Inner Harmonies of this Universe must always be the highest glory for a man, and not to know always the highest disgrace for a man, however common it be." To constrain men to think of God: what He is, what He thinks and purposes in all His working, how He feels

SOCIAL WORSHIP. 23

towards men who hate and despise themselves for their sins; to proclaim the living God, the God of law and right, and mercy and good; this is the preacher's work, and this work effectively done, social worship at once takes its place as the primary agent in the cultivation and enrichment of the spiritual life of the world. Well may we ask with Emerson—

What greater calamity can fall upon a nation than the loss of worship? Then all things go to decay. Genius leaves the temple, to haunt the senate, or the market. Literature becomes frivolous. Science is cold. The eye of youth is not lighted by the hope of other worlds, and age is without honour. Society lives to trifles, and when men die, we do not mention them.

Not such is our fate. "Walk about Zion." Recall the service of our sanctuaries to the life of the nation. Estimate the spiritual manhood reared in the village communion and the town church. See the springheads of the people's best life, and resolve to maintain the social worship of our sanctuaries pure and real, glowing and reverent, and above all rich in vital speech concerning the redemption of men in Christ Jesus, and so tell to the generation following that this "God revealed in the Gospel of Jesus is our God for ever and ever, and that He will be our guide even unto death."

Delphi proved false to the trust that had been committed to her. She sought wealth and power. She gave to a party what was meant for mankind. She cared more for pomp and show than spiritual power, and it became her ruin, and the Greek world lost its religious centre and its religious inspiration.

Zion proved false to her trust. It knew not the day of its visitation. It allowed itself to be blinded by prejudice and pride, cared more for orthodoxy than for souls, became avaricious where it should have been selfless, stood upon the dignity of its orders instead of doing its true work, claimed pre-eminence, panted "to go in long clothing, loved salutations in the market place, chief seats in the synagogues, and the uppermost rooms at feasts," instead of making itself of no reputation and being obedient in all things and at all times to the law of God; and therefore Zion became desolate, and not one stone was left upon another.

It is a solemn responsibility. Preach Christ, the revelation of the Father, the way, the truth, and the life; preach Christ through whom we have the forgiveness of sins, and the life, that is life indeed; but, above all, and through all, seek with all your hearts the grace that will enable you to manifest the spirit of Christ in your public worship and in your daily life.

God the Home of the Soul.

"Lord, Thou hast been our dwelling-place in all generations."—PSALM XC. 1.

1. *The Home.*

As is a mother to her babe, so is God to us. *She* makes the children's home—not the two-roomed cottage of the peasant, with the bare walls and scant furniture, nor the many-roomed ducal palace, with its teeming wealth and oppressive luxury; but the love and light, the warm kisses and tender care, the sweet smile and the strong soul of the mother —she, and all that she is, makes "*Home*, sweet, sweet Home." She is the dwelling-place of the child's heart, the satisfaction of desire, the unfailing nourishment of the child's life. What God has made that mother to her child, He Himself is to us men, our asylum of peace, our refuge from passing foes, our dwelling-place and home from age to age.

Young Augustine, like the prodigal of our Saviour's parable, and like many of us, began his new life with the discovery of this, the deepest fact of all our life, and from a heart scorched with sin and fevered with evil passions there broke out the word, as fathomless in meaning as it is familiar, as full of pathos as of daring in its outleap of faith, "Thou hast made us for Thyself." "Made *us*," although blackened by sin, foul with evil desire, maddened by repeated rebellions, "made us for Thyself, and we are restless till we rest in Thee." That discovery, which re-made Augustine in the fourth century, was, like so many other discoveries, no more than the re-discovery of the truths that had been the strength and hope and joy of Israel centuries before, when, gazing upon the stable hills and unchanging mountains, the cry broke forth from the sore and bruised heart, "Thou hast been the dwelling-place of Thy people in all generations."

It is a song of faith and venture. Like the bird that seems as though it would burst its little throat with its piercing music after it has escaped the frowning eye of the hawk, so this singer facing the loneliness and sorrow, the pinched resources and wasting life of his fellows, refuses to yield to the spasms of doubt that have just gone shattering through his soul, and breaks forth in a hymn of adoring trust in the Creator of the everlasting mountains as the abiding refuge of his spirit. Stirred by suffering, and forecasting swiftly approaching disaster, he takes hold on God. Calm strength returns, he is girded anew for the strife, and filled with undimmed hope. For God is the soul's real home.

2. *The Father.*

Many know the mountains, and wander over them measuring their heights, and, perhaps awestruck by their grandeur, but never hear from them any message concerning their home in the Eternal: "God is not in all their thoughts." They believe in God, but not as they do in the hills. They dwell in the world of sense; but He is the Father of spirits, and is within us and around us. We live in Him. He invests us. He

glows above
With scarce an intervention, presses close
And palpitatingly, His soul o'er ours.

He "is Love, and he that dwelleth in God dwelleth in Love," and love is life. When a little Boston girl who had been blind, deaf, and dumb till she was eleven years of age, was at length led by Phillips Brooks to understand that God made the world and us, that He was willing to be to us a Father if we would only take the place of children, and that Jesus had given His life to bring us back to God; she said in her artless way, "Yes, I knew that before, but I didn't know His name." So before men had found the way to her mind through the senses God had spoken with His quiet voice within. He tells us much before we know His name. He finds us and talks to us if we have ears to hear. We only need to "practise the presence of God" by practising the vital element of love, and we shall know Him whom to know is life everlasting.

But God also is righteousness, and "he that keepeth His commandments dwelleth in God and God in him." We are not far from the very feet of God when we are doing or bearing His will. If the good we did yesterday is followed by better to-day and the best to-morrow, it is because our Father is graciously inspiring and training us. We are dwelling in the heavenlies. We aspire. Excelsior is in our heart. We are restful as God Himself; but we are too earnest for indolence, and too aspiring for complete content. So in the ways of obedience we are always hearing some new message, seeing life in some new setting, responding to some new call, or starting on some fresh march against the foe.

3. *The Family.*

The soul that talks to God rises out of a narrow and selfish individualism into fellowship, not only with the Eternal Creator, but also with the vast and various family of God in the past, present, and future. We are dwelling in the same home as our fathers and brothers and sons. Israel is there in its completeness. God is the eternal home of the race. "The elders who, through faith, obtained a good report," in the grey dawn of the world, dwelt therein. Abraham, Isaac, and Jacob, the founders of Israel, had long since passed away, but their home was not broken up, for they still lived in and to God. Indeed, all our dead live in Him, for He is not the God of dead men, but of living men, for all live unto Him. Thus we are already all together with the Lord. Arthur Neale, like Bunyan's Mr. Fearing, was "kept very low, and made his life burdensome to himself" by fear of death. But as he came near to his end his fear disappeared, and "he went over at last not much above wet-shod," sending, as his last message to his friends, the brave words, "Tell them all, it's all right!"

Can we have any surer key to unlock the past? Clouds of darkness are round about the beginnings of our race, and scarcely does the cloud lift or the darkness disappear as the race advances through struggle and battle. But the past should not be our burden. That is God's. We cannot touch it save as the schoolboy his lesson book. Why, then, should its problems crush us? Rather should we be occupied with our immediate duty. Let the past inspire us to sing :

Build thee more stately mansions, O my soul,
　As the swift seasons roll!
　Leave thy low-vaulted past
Let each new temple, nobler than the last,
Shut thee from heaven with a dome more vast,
　Till thou at length art free,
Leaving thine outgrown shell by life's unresting sea!

4. *The Fellowship.*

The home is the place of communion, of the interchange of confidences, of the fellowship of spirit with spirit. It is the atmosphere in which prayer is born, and in which the praying spirit may utter itself freely, frankly, and not be afraid. As a mother quickens the desires and lifts the aspirations of the child, so God urges us forward to holier deed and deeper devotion, and will not let us rest in our pitiable brokenness and weakening sins. He pleads within us, as well as teaches us, and begets hunger for holiness, and struggle for the infinite Beauty. God broods in, rules over us, and wins us to deep content with His eternal will, and cheers and heals us by His presence.

As a sick child puts out its hand in the dark night and is soothed when it rests on its mother's bosom, so our sorrows become sacred and our troubles free our speech. He bears our infirmities and carries our sorrows; and they who are weak are made strong by feeling that He is near, and that

He knows all, and will hear and answer the prayer,

Oh, empty us of self, the world and sin,
And then in all Thy fulness enter in.

This is our present peace. *We shall be like Him, for we shall see Him as He is:* and though we cannot trace the full effects of the present fellowship, yet it is certain that we are being transformed by it after the likeness of God. The home influence is all-pervasive. It abides. It enters into our being as a formative force, and so we pass from glory to glory as by the Spirit of the Lord. All is not lost: we shall be like Him. Let us hope on, and be steadfast in the faith that "the Will of God is bearing all things that yield to it to the joy of their Lord."

How Paul Thought of the Incarnation.

WE all want to know how to think rightly of the Incarnation.

At the beginning, the birth of Jesus was declared to be "good tidings of great joy to all people"; and, howsoever we may view that epoch-making event, it has been a source of hope and a fountain of delight to many. It was to the aged Simeon, who, when waiting for the consolation of Israel, saw in the Wonderful Babe, brought by Mary into the Temple, the realisation of his fondest anticipations for Israel and for the world. It was to Anna, the saintly prophetess, who, at the sight of the same God - sent Visitor, gave thanks, and bade all who were looking for the redemption of

THE INCARNATION. 37

Jerusalem be of good courage and wait on the Lord.

And to thousands since those early days the Advent of Jesus has been the most welcome and inspiring of gospels. It has helped us to think that "the All-Great" is the "All-Loving" too; and

> So, through the thunder of our life has come a human voice,
> Saying, "O heart I made, a heart beats here!
> Face, My hands fashioned, see it in Myself;
> Thou hast no power nor may'st conceive of Mine,
> But love I gave thee, with Myself to love,
> And thou must love Me who have died for thee!"

But whether the Incarnation is, or is not, good news to us depends upon how we think of it; what answer we give to the questions, "Who was Jesus, and whence came He? Why did He come when He did, and not earlier or later? In Palestine and not in London? In the first and not in the nineteenth century? For what purpose did He come, and what has His coming accomplished for us men?"

Such questions are irrepressible. For their answers concern the very soul and substance of the Christian religion, the true interpretation of history, the solution of the riddle of human life, the removal of the burden of sin, the discovery and vindication of the plan of God in His rule of the world, the forecast of the predestined goal of our race, and the full explanation of the universe, and of its Creator and Ruler. Therefore, we cannot refuse to face the inquiry, "How ought we to think about the Incarnation so as to think truly, and according to the reality and fulness, of the fact as it was and is?"

To that inquiry Paul gives one comprehensive and luminous answer when writing to the Galatians, within a quarter of a century of the death of the Founder of Christianity.

First, he tells us, the Incarnation is a predestined event in the furtherance of the redemption and education of humanity. It occurs in the "fulness of the time." That is the primary fact. It is not an accident. It is part of, and fits into, a fully articulated plan of world - redemption. It closes an epoch. It opens a new era. It is not a separable accident, cut off from the rest of the life of the race; it is an integral part of it, with vital relations to its earliest manifestations, and to its latest, and to each and every experience of man between the first and the last. It is no afterthought. It happens just when it ought to happen, when it was meant to happen, when it could take its place and do its work most effectively. The time receptacle into which the centuries and millenniums had been poured was full up to the precise moment when this great event should be added; and it was added just then. The fixings in God's calendar were kept. The administration of the world was, and is, a perfectly organised system, fixed and secured in all its parts, forming a symmetrical and harmonious whole. It is not a series of disconnected forces and events. Each fact is a cause and a consequent, a link in the chain of continuous action, and is held and also holds. Each force works with all the forces, and all the forces with each towards a predestined end.

We can easily see for ourselves *now* what Paul saw then. In God's World-School the time had arrived for the advent of the New Teacher with His next set of lessons. Man was no longer an infant. The animal struggle was

OF THE INCARNATION. 41

not in any sense ended; but he had learnt fear and faith, wonder and reverence, love and hope, and was hungering in intellect and in conscience for further revelations. The Jew's long training found voice in one piercing but confused cry to God for deliverance. Taught by Abraham and Moses, by prophet and seer, in Egypt and in Babylon, he stood alone in his overwhelming sense of the heinousness of sin and his intense passion for righteousness. He saw, as few others did, what John Morley calls "the catastrophe of sin," and he was looking for a Teacher who should be, as the best teacher always is, a Redeemer. In Greece man had been taught the value of truth, the love of veracity, and the service of the reason; and by the universal distribution of the Greek language, the nations of the earth were prepared for recognising not only the Hebrew message, but that fuller statement of the same message in Christ Jesus given by His disciples. Finally, Roman ambition had just welded the various states of the world into one kingdom, so that the heralds of the Cross could march on Roman roads and under Roman protection, preaching to all the nations the Gospel of God. It was "the fulness of the time." Everywhere the cry was being heard, "Lift up the gates, and be ye lift up ye everlasting doors, and the King of Glory shall come in."

And He came! At that moment of clamant need and supreme advantage "God sent forth His Son"—"His only-begotten and well-beloved Son"; sent Him forth from His "bosom," as John expresses it, when suggesting the deep and loving intimacies from which Jesus enters our strange and sinful life; "sent Him forth, *born of a woman*," sharing the lowliness of our ordinary entrance into life as well as its deepest and saddest conditions, its limitations and crudenesses, its temptations and sorrows. The Incarnation is, indeed, God Himself coming into our humanity in the very fulness of His redemptive love and grace, and assuming its total conditions, so that He may make an end of sin and bring in an everlasting righteousness. That is its deepest meaning according to the mind of Paul. God completes the redemption and education of the world Himself, in His actual Person; not by sending forth a bolder Elijah or a more seraphic Isaiah, but by sending forth Himself; if I may say it, the dearest portion of Himself—" His Son." Paul's chief thought of the Incarnation is that it is a special and unique entrance of God into humanity. That is its essence. There lies its meaning and power. God was in Christ, and Christ was in our life, in the whole of it;

starting with its lowliest beginnings and continuing throughout its course, in order to complete the redemptive purpose of the Eternal. Christmas is Emmanuel, God with us; God Himself with us; God, the true God, seen in Him who is true, *i.e.*, in Jesus—seen as He is in His innermost being and thought and purpose and work.

For, to Paul the Incarnation is always redemptive. Jesus was "born under the law to redeem them that were under the law." Paul could not think of the Incarnation as a fact apart from the work of Christ as Redeemer. It was not a separate interest from the Cross. It was the Cross. He could not give it a place beneath or above the Atonement, as less inclusive or less central and fundamental. Jesus was one, and the whole of His life and work is redemptive. The birth in Bethlehem is not to be isolated from the death on Calvary, and one set over against the other as though they were not parts of one and the same great whole. The unity of the ages is repeated in the unity of the Redemptive life and work of the Saviour. The Incarnation is as sacrificial and atoning as is the Cross. It is, indeed, the Atonement itself beginning at the lowest rounds of our human life, entering in at lowly doors, making itself of no reputation, becoming obedient to the conditions which bear the Saviour straight to the Cross and to the Eternal Throne. Alas! how the "Creeds" have fallen short of the great conceptions of Paul! They emphasize the unimportant and obtrude the insignificant. They lack the glorious breadth and compass of the Apostle. It would be an infinite gain to Christendom if we could get back to the depth and grandeur, the wholeness and harmony, of Pauline thinking on the Advent of Jesus.

But the capital charm of Paul's thought of the Incarnation is that, besides being the fullest entrance of God into our humanity, it is also the advent of the Spirit of sonship to God into human hearts. Jesus redeems us from a life of slavery to outward and mechanical rules of living, terminates our subjection to external authority, to rite and custom, and gives us the freedom and joy, the largeness and strength of consciously reconciled and happy sons of God. He introduces an era of sonship—repeating in us, and making supreme in our consciousness, as it is in Jesus Himself, the sense of our filial relationship to the Father. He makes us feel "at home" with God, so that the thought of Him is a joy, a delight, an altogether gladdening and enlarging uplift to the soul. That is the message of Christmas. God is not far away from any one of us. He is near us, with the free offer of His full forgiveness. We have been prodigal, we have wasted our life and the lives of others; let us return and say, "Father, I have sinned against heaven and in Thy sight; I am no more worthy to be called Thy son," and God, who has waited longingly for our return, will embrace us, and we shall hear the welcoming song, "Bring forth quickly the best robe and put it on him, and put a ring on his hand and shoes on his feet; and bring the fatted calf and kill it, and let us eat and make merry, for this my son was dead and is alive again; he was lost and is found."

Jesus Praying.

"These things spake Jesus; and lifting up His eyes to heaven, he said, Father, the hour is come; glorify Thy Son, that the Son may glorify Thee: even as Thou gavest Him authority over all flesh, that whatsoever Thou hast given Him, to them He should give eternal life. And this is life eternal, that they should know Thee the only true God, and Him whom thou didst send, *even* Jesus Christ."
JOHN XVII. 1, 2, 3.

JOHN KNOX, on the day before his death, and when the vision of the opening gate of eternity was becoming more and more clear, called his wife and said to her, "Go, read where I cast my first anchor," and so she read to him the seventeenth chapter of John's Gospel. And as he listened to the calm yet fervent pleadings of the Saviour of men, he was rescued from the tossings of an inward sea; his faith was reinforced, and he felt that strange, unearthly peace which is one token of the gracious presence of the Redeemer Himself.

In the days of his ministry in the chapel of the Castle of St. Andrews, Knox had taught the people, day by day, from the treasures of John's evangel; and now, at last, the bold but troubled spirit of the Great Reformer finds fresh anchorage in this solid and irremovable rock, where he had, in the beginning of his spiritual history, "cast his first anchor."

Spener, the German Pietist, and a contemporary of the saintly Fénelon, and breathing the same devoutness, as he lay dying, asked that this same prayer might be read to him once and twice, and even a third time, and then said, "Although this chapter had always been peculiarly dear to him, he had never been willing to preach from it, because he had never understood it, and thought that the full understanding of it transcended the measure of faith which the Lord was wont to dispense to His people in the days of their pilgrimage."

Both Knox and Spener are dying, and both feel the mystic charm of this most precious Scripture; but they are not drawn to it in the same mood, nor with the same purpose. Spener, the man of meditation and prayer, asks to hear afresh the intercessions of the Son of God, so that he may make one more effort to fathom their significance, breathe their spirit, and find at last, if it should be possible, the interpreting faith which he thinks has been denied to him hitherto. But the fighting Reformer, the man of bold words and brave deeds, who was the friend of truth and the foe of frauds, is drawn to it as a sick child to the mother's bosom; as the hungry, weary, and worn-out pilgrim to a friendly fireside. It is for him a haven of refuge, a home for the wanderer, "the shadow of a great rock in a weary land."

Were Knox and Spener alone in their witness to the spell cast over the hearts and minds of men by this matchless prayer, their testimony would be worth more than gold, were it of the finest quality and the largest quantity; but these fighting, praying men, for they were both—fighting men are mostly praying men, and praying men ought always to be fighting men—I say these fighting, praying men are only two of the vast brotherhood of reflective, patient, warring souls who have borne the burden and heat of life with a deepened serenity, and a more heroic steadfastness, because they have watched the face, and heard the voice, of Jesus as He talked to His Father on that night in which He was betrayed.

As the 23rd Psalm has been like an angel of God, uttering its message of cheer and gladness to many a sorrowing soul, quickening faculty, inspiring faith, giving sweetness to life, and relieving death of its terrors; so the 17th of John has been as a prophet of the Highest, meeting us in the hard and lonely places of life, helping us to take up and carry our cross with unconquerable soul, to be tranquil in the fell clutch of circumstance, and to finish our most exacting work without breach of faithfulness to God and duty.

For, first, *it is a source of intellectual rest to see Jesus in prayer*, and to listen to the tender pleading tones of His supplications. Sometimes we are tempted to ask —who indeed is not?—is it worth while to pray? Can it do any good? Isn't this an ordered universe, based on law, administered in obedience to law by One who is Himself the Law-maker and Law-giver, and the very fountain of all order, and who is not likely to have left room to deviate from His regulations in compliance with the expression of our confused and bewildered desires? Is He not bound in chains so inexorable that all asking and receiving are absolutely and for ever shut out?

So it often seems, and yet He prays; and therefore I may. He, the Son of the Father, who comes from the bosom of the Father, from the deepest intimacies of the Divine, who knew the Father as no one else ever can—He prays, not once or twice, as if by accident, but often and long, and specially and with much feeling, in the crises of His work and mission.

> Cold mountains and the midnight air
> Witnessed the fervour of His prayer.

He prays—for Himself: that He as the Son of the Father may be glorified—prays for Himself first, and says He prays: "I pray"—prays for His disciples—

for their safety in the midst of evil; and prays for the great succession of disciples to the end of the world. He, the only-begotten Son of the Father, His best beloved Son because His best, His most obedient, His perfectly obedient Son, He prays and therefore I may, therefore I will.

I cannot answer all the curious questions of the brain, concerning Prayer and Law; not half of them, indeed; and I will not attempt it; but, like Knox, I will cast my anchor here, in this revealing fact that He, the Holiest of the holy and the Wisest of the wise, He prays: therefore I am assured this anchorage of Divine example will hold the vessel in the tossings of the wildest sea of doubt, and that I shall be safe as He was if the vessel itself is engulfed in the waves of suffering and sorrow. His act is an argument. His prayer is an inspiration. His achievements are the everlasting and all-sufficient vindication of prayer.

But secondly, it is *a revelation of the truest sources of moral power to see Jesus the Son of God, in communion with His Father in this the chiefest crisis of His life.* Indeed, it is this urgent need of immediate help he puts in the very foreground as His plea for praying at all. Each opening word indicated the hunger of His soul for strength. He says, "Father, the hour is come." He is a child, and a child in sore trouble, and to whom should He go if not to His Father? And what should He do in this dark day if not talk to Him and tell all He feels and hopes and endures? The relation vindicates the fullest, freest speech, invites the most outspoken confidence. He is the Son of the Father; come from His bosom, and come to do His will; has found His meat, His very life and its nourishment in this close and most endearing relation; and therefore with a naturalness that is itself an argument, He begins in this dark night with the word, so sweet, so strong, so revealing, " Father, the great dread hour has come; hold Thou Me up; keep Me true, help and glorify Thy Son."

It is not a stranger who speaks; it is a son. The suppliant does not call from a distance as to a vague and formless infinite; but to a Father, His Father, His own Father, who loves Him and delights in Him and in His work. It is not a son engaged in a task to which his father is averse or strange; it is the work which the Father Himself has given Him to do, and has been preparing to get done throughout all preceding generations. It was therefore inevitable at such a time of peril as this that Father and Son should come together, and that once more should be heard the cry, " Father, glorify Thy Son," and the welcome response ring deep and full in the soul of Jesus, "I have both glorified Thee, and will glorify Thee again."

Brothers, we cannot think rightly about prayer unless we conceive of ourselves as sons of God. Forget that capital, central fact, and prayer is a mystery you cannot fathom; remember it, and it is as natural as warmth on a midsummer's day, and greetings and good wishes with the opening year. Place yourself amongst the stones and rocks of the geologist, the salts and acids of the chemist, or the flowers and trees of the botanist, and you will not see any place for prayer. Remember that you are souls related to the Eternal Soul—not distantly, but closely —most closely, even as sons to a Father who loves His children so much that He will suffer anything for their salvation, and then, prayer, as the free interchange of thought and love, will be the most natural and befitting act in which you can engage. Prayer is the love-talk of the family, of son with father and of a father with his son. Jesus, who is the authentic revelation of man, of his relation to the universe and to its Maker and Ruler, of his inmost consciousness and possibilities, assures us in His pattern sonship that in our most sorrowful hours we may approach Him who has made us, confident that He will not turn away from our prayer nor reject the voice of our supplication.

But there is more in the Saviour's opening words, as a plea for prayer, as a source of spiritual power, than this fact of Fatherhood and its correlative of sonship. Jesus says, "The hour is come," the long-dreaded hour; the hour of portent and disaster is in sight; the hour of unutterable perils is at last here; that is enough! No further plea is needed. The burdened Son therefore names it, and forthwith pours out His supreme desires, His deepest wishes in His Father's ear, and then rises and goes forward to His cross as one who has already conquered. He gets all He wants, the "strength" to bear up and on, and go right forward, undeterred by paroxysms of pain, unappalled by accumulated opposition, and undaunted by the scoffs and hatred and malignity of men; offering Himself as a sacrifice to make an end of the sin, the cruelty, the rebellion, and the folly of the world.

It was strength He wanted, and that was all He wanted. On that His heart was set, and He gained it, not taking the kingdom of heaven by violence, but by patience; not by the force of His attack, but by the power of communion with His Father, thereby winning for others as well as for Himself the great grace of enriching the Divine life that flows into and through the world. Now could a son in such a case have done better or wiser? Could He have discovered the courage and patience to obey unto death, even the death of the cross, more swiftly or more surely? Is it not the one true and living way of strength for those critical hours of our life in which every moment seems to be charged with destiny? Is it not, too, the way the sons of God have instinctively trod and made luminous for ever by their victorious march?

For all lives have their highest points. Human existence is not a dead level, monotonous and flat as the scenery of Cambridgeshire. It is more like the landscapes of Scotland or Switzerland. It has its vales and hills, its retreating coves, and its heaven-soaring peaks; and the sons and daughters of God will call out to their Father when they reach those heights. It is on Mount Moriah Abraham hears the voice of the Eternal and achieves his heroic surrender of himself and his son to his God. It is in his selection of the den of lions in preference to the steps of the throne of a king that Daniel comes into closest communion with Jehovah. It is Luther who counts no time lost that is given to prayer, who is the conqueror at the Diet of Worms.

So for us the darkness of a sleepless night has been less oppressive because we have talked with God, and the burden of the day has been less heavy to bear because our secret souls have communed with Him who bids us cast our care upon Him, for He careth for us. I was told the other day that in Ceylon, where the sun's heat is scorchingly hot at mid-day, the birds, seeking shelter from the oppressive heat, sit in rows along the lines of shade made on the grass by the telegraph wires and telegraph poles. It is but a slight shadow, but they welcome it; so from the burning heat of life some of us have sought and found relief, as we have sat in the shadow of the prayer-meeting, or of the common prayer of the Sabbath-day. If souls are sympathetic with God, very much in earnest in doing His work, and can enter with intense trust and warm heart into communion with the Father, then their great spiritual issues cannot fail; though they go down to the grave they will rise again, and the deepest point of their humiliation will be the beginning of their Divine ascent.

But, thirdly, *we must know what Jesus asks for if we are to discover the fullest justification of prayer.* Remember where Jesus is; get as accurately as you can at the contents of that supreme hour, of which He speaks, and then hear Him say, "Glorify Thy Son, that the Son may glorify Thee; that as Thou hast given Him authority over all flesh, He may use all

Thou hast given Him so as to bring to men the blessing of life, life for evermore."

Jesus prays that He may perfectly finish His work of redemption, and leave it without flaw; that He may be able to be obedient to the very end of His alloted task, and so reveal Himself in His true character, and thereby show what God Himself is—what God wills, and what man, inspired and filled with God, may be and do; and thus testify to all men the utmost each man may have from God, and all that each man may become and may do by the grace of God.

So Jesus pushes forward His own will, clings to it tenaciously, and urges it, says distinctly what He wants, not as one feeling that he is in the presence of irrevocable law, and that no wish is possible except that in the cry, "Thy will be done"; and that there can be no prayer but the prayer of silence.

No; He asks for glory; for glory for Himself.

But it is not a selfish prayer; not a prayer for ease, for deliverance, or for fame and repute as men judge them, but for the "glory"—that is to say, for the reputation, with its accompanying splendours, which genuine character and worthy achievement win in the eyes of intelligent beings. For a man's greatest victory is to compel a recognition of his true character. Christ had been misunderstood, maligned, misrepresented, thwarted, hindered in His service to men and in His mission for God; and therefore He is asking that He may be able to reveal Himself in these tragical circumstances exactly as He is, and so being lifted up on the cross may draw all men to Him, compel them to gaze on the Divine reality, and know God just for what He is and for what He has come to do; therefore He says, "Suffer Me not for any pains of death to fall from Thee" and from my vocation. Keep me true to the last, faithful to the end: uphold Me, Father, that I may crown the revelation I have given of Thee in life, in and by My death." Up to this point all that Jesus could do to make God known He had done. It was His "name" He had manifested to His followers, so that they might know of a truth that he came forth from God, and believe that He was sent forth by Him. It was in that "name" or revelation of God His disciples were to be kept as in an enchanted ground; it only remained that He should complete the demonstration of what lay at the back of His teaching and of His deeds, by His unmurmuring patience in the garden, and His steadfast obedience on the cross.

Thus the Son, sustained by the Father, would add to the splendours of the Divine name, unfold the contents of the revelation of God, glorify the Divine character, and make life, God's life, spirit, energy, power, grace, righteousness, patience, and love, the available possession of all; even that life eternal, which begins in knowing God, as He really is and feels, and wishes and rules, and in knowing Jesus Christ whom He has sent; and then advances to its predestined goal by our enjoying, as an actual and conscious possession, the fulness of His Divine Spirit.

Given, then, a son of man who realises that he is a son of God, and has received a commission from his Father to declare His name, that is, to reveal His character, to set it forth in all its splendour and magnetic power: add to that this, that the revelation is to be made in conditions of intolerable pain and cruelty, and by the total eclipse of self, what is more likely or fitting than that he should lift up his eyes to Heaven, and say, "Father, help me; hold Thou my hand"?

Say what you will, and what you may, I cannot refuse to think that reason, the highest, most perfected reason, could not find out a wiser or more conquering course. The highest manhood ever lived vindicates it. The greatest victories ever won, even those of Calvary, justify it. Therefore we pray.

> O Thou, by whom we come to God,
> The Life, the Truth, the Way,
> The path of prayer Thyself hast trod,
> Lord, teach us how to pray.

And suppose He answers that prayer, how shall we know the answer when it comes? In these ways.

If He send into us the spirit of adoption wherein we cry, Father, Father, knowing something of the sweet and powerful significance of the gracious appellation—if He possess us with a passion, deep, full and strong, for the redemption of men by the revealing of God to men; so that we are ready to use whatever authority or power, or gift or possession, we may have in such a way as to persuade, yea, compel men to see the true character of God and open their hearts to the advent of His Spirit.

We say, let us save men, let us evangelise the world, let us send the missionary to the ends of the earth; and we say well, provided we do not forget that the cry really means, "Let us show God as He is, really is in Himself, to men; show what we know is His glory, His reputation with added splendour; even His work of redemption and reconciliation by Jesus Christ." If Jesus teaches us how to pray, that will be our desire, our one strong and unquenchable enthusiasm, for which we will die or live.

And, lastly, if Jesus teaches us to pray, the passion to be true to

God in our thought and deed, and thereby to reveal Him, will be so strong in us that we shall suffer anything, endure anything, and gladly take the loss of all things rather than misrepresent Him! In the hour that is blackest and darkest in our life we shall say, Father, don't suffer me to play the coward; make me willing to endure the cross, to despise the shame, to reject all pleasure, and render all service, only that I may do Thy will and thereby reveal Thy character and mind to men. So glorify Thy child, that Thy child may add to the faith, the love, the purity, the sweetness, the strength, and the righteousness of the world.

The Church of the Ages.

"I will thank Jehovah with my whole heart in the council and assembly of the upright."
—PSALM cxi.

1. *Its Signs.*

THERE can be little doubt concerning the place of this psalm, and the one that follows it, in the life of Israel. In literary structure, in contents, and in purpose, they remind us of the "Wisdom Literature" of the Old Testament, and offer the same features and topics as those presented in the books of *Proverbs* and *Job* and in *Psalms I., II., XXXVII.,* and *CXIX.*

This is a joy-song about the fellowship of the saints, a sweet strain of music chanted by one of those "who feared the Lord and spake often to one another" concerning His law, His leadings, and His exceeding great and precious promises to His people. It is the inspired hymn of the Watts or Bonar of the Exile Church. But there is an undertone of sadness in its lines. For it is a dark and cloudy day, and the Psalmist feels the chill of loneliness, and the pain and numbness of accumulated defeats and disappointments. Princes have persecuted him and his fellows without cause, and the proud have made a mockery of their religion. The great hope of a coming deliverer is under eclipse. The opiates of despair are always within reach. Long and patiently have they waited for the dawn, and as the weak, helpless, and sleepless invalid watches for the morning light, so have they listened for the voice of the herald announcing the advent of the servant of the Lord; and still the night is cold and dark.

Nevertheless, "Unto the upright there ariseth light in the darkness," and it ariseth from the congregation of believing and undespairing men. The Church of the Holy is a fountain of perennial hope. Like a lighthouse to a shipwrecked mariner, so by the Church he finds his way to safety and to song. In its light he sees light. The Church, like the God who made it and rules it, "is a very present help in trouble."

The wide expanses of Israel's history, luminous with exceeding great and precious promises, are studied therein. There the voice of the living God is heard, and the presence of the living God is felt; there that reverence for Him and His words and works, which is the beginning and the end of all wise living, grows from more to more, so that "mind and heart according well made one music as before, but vaster"; and there, above all, is revealed that

THE CHURCH OF THE AGES. 73

righteousness which seen in God is the strength of our hearts and our portion for ever; and when achieved in ourselves is the proof of our participation in His nature, the supreme charm and glory of the council of the upright, and the most cogent witness for God amongst the sons of men.

2. *Its Fellowship.*

The note with which the poem starts is that of glowing and grateful appreciation of the Church. The singer rejoices in "the council of the upright," in the congregation of those who seek for righteousness. His burdened soul is at home there. The congenial atmosphere attracts him, inspires him, cheers him. There his friends dwell, and in their society he forgets that he is a stranger and a wanderer. Therefore will he give thanks to God with his whole heart.

There is a kinship far closer than that of the flesh, and there are bonds of the spirit sweeter and stronger than all those of intellect and fancy, of society and service. The soul is the man; and when soul recognises soul in communion, all the finer qualities of our nature are developed, and the deeper life, the life of humility and holiness, the life that roots itself in God, becomes stronger and stronger. George Bowen says: "Men are fully aware of the advantage of partnerships. They even form partnerships for the prosecution of some labours that would seem most likely to be well performed by a single individual: as, for example, the labours of authorship. But they are not aware that any gain would result from entering into partnership with the promises of God as their capital and the Throne of Grace as their place of business. Our Lord teaches that association in prayer is so exceedingly profitable, that even if two only should embark in it there would be grand results. Let three, four, or a hundred and twenty of one accord, of one mind, seek to utilise the promises; commensurate fruit shall appear in some early day of Pentecost. The great thing is not the numbers, but the agreement. The prayer of two whose souls are attuned to exactly the same key, and who have learned to merge their separate interests in one common interest, shall prevail more than the prayers of ten thousand whose minds and hearts are occupied more or less with lingering considerations of purely personal good." It is this agreement our Psalmist feels. It is to give thanks to God with his whole heart in their presence he purposes. His desire for God makes him seek the freest, purest spirits he can find. He wants the society of those who will feed his fervours, guide his studies of God and of His works, and inspire his worship. It is not the council of the wealthy or even of the favoured, but of the upright: it is not the congregation of the learned or of the orthodox, but of those whose hearts are set on the doing of His holy law. He does not wish to encounter influences hostile to faith and love and joy; but to dwell where the atmosphere, or "climate," nourishes high ideals, heroic venture, holy aspirations, intense and impartial love, and pure and steadfast service. The real test of a church is in the quality of the spirits it attracts to itself, not simply in its numbers or in its wealth or fame.

3. *Its Studies.*

The charm and power of the society of the upright is described in two other features (v. 2); first in the natural and instinctive joy its members feel in the wonderful activities of the living God; and secondly in the concerted and devoted investigation of those works. They take pleasure in the works of God. They welcome His appearing, exult in His manifested holiness and mercy, and delight greatly in His whole administration of the life of man. As a display of power and wisdom, it attracts and cheers the soul, fills it with adoring worship, and inspires it with unconquerable hope.

"The works of the Lord are great," "studied," sought out, discovered, examined and described in their relations and revelations by all those who delight in God. And, therefore, they gather themselves together, in order that they may prosecute their studies with avidity and with success, and under conditions that aid keenness of sight and grasp of mind. They follow on to know the Lord. They seek to realise His lovingkindness in His temple, to know what it is, to trace its workings, to experience its healing of the heart and cleansing of the mind, to see how it interprets the past, and prepares for the future; and thereby to be able to say " Return unto thy rest, O my soul, for the Lord hath dealt bountifully with thee." Praise is thus deepened and purified by knowledge. Adoration grows by study of the great and glorious acts of God in the redemption and renewal of His people. Faith works by study in the radiant atmosphere of the Church, and so brings light, calm: and the soul sings—

Not, Lord, Thine ancient works alone,
Thy wonders to past ages shown,
   Make our glad spirits glow.
Our eyes behold Thy works of might;
On us full beam Thy wonders bright;
   The living God we know.

4. *Its Solace.*

The first feature of the Divine activity mentioned by the singer is its glory and splendour. "Glorious and grand is His doing," or "Glory and splendour is His work" (v. 3). The beauty of the flowers and of the landscape, bathed in golden sunshine; the magnificence and sublimity of the uprising mountains, the brilliancy of the starry sky; and still more the mighty deeds of deliverance of the people of God from their oppressors; the grant to them of the heritage of the heathen; the unique manifestations of the Divine favour; these are the themes which invite and reward the student's research, and fill the devout heart with praise and love.

The heavens declare the glory of God,
And the firmament showeth His handiwork.

So the work of God has stirred the soul of man to thought, and reverence, and awe, to trust and praise.

But the brilliance and splendour of the Creation and Providence of God are surpassed by that righteousness of His which endureth for ever. It is this brings to man a true and abiding peace. The Lord is a God of judgment, or, as the seventh and eighth verses say, amplifying this phase of the Divine activities—

The works of His hands are truth and justice,
All His behests are worthy of faith,
They are established eternally and for ever,
Wrought out in truth and in uprightness.

The wise saw God as the God of truth and order, of law and method, of inflexible justice and love; a ruler of men who "laid down His lines according to righteousness, and established His laws in wisdom," and remained for generations always consistent with them. "It is a great truth," says Prof. G. Adam Smith, "that the Almighty and All-merciful is the

All-methodical, too; and no religion is complete in its creed, or healthy in its influence, which does not insist equally on all three."

It is here man, seemingly the sport of contrary forces and the victim of hidden energies, finds his rest. He is assured that "the Lord will wait, that He may be gracious unto us; and therefore will He be exalted that He may have mercy upon us," for the Lord is a God of method. Blessed are all they that wait for Him.

Not the peace that the world gives—

Nor peace that grows by Lethe, scentless flower,
  There in white languors to decline and cease;
But peace whose names are also rapture, power,
  Clear sight and love; for those are parts of peace!

Let not your hearts be troubled, believe in God. He waits that He may be gracious. He is the God of Truth, and all His works are wrought in orderly fashion and on the basis of absolute justice. "He never is before His time, and never is too late." Praise ye the Lord.

5. *Its Memorial.*

To this permanence of righteousness the divinely ordered life of Israel bore witness. The recurring festivals propagated the remembrance of the deeds of God in the Mosaic ages and in the times of the Judges and of the Kings; the deeds of glory and of splendour, the acts of righteousness and truth; and proclaimed the eternal truth that God is a God of pity, as well as strength; that forgiveness is a part of His established order, and redemption His deepest delight.

"A Memorial has He made for His wonders." He has inspired

and ordered the setting apart of a special time and of specially commemorative feasts, recalling the manna that fell in the wilderness, the quails that met the hunger of the complaining pilgrims; the deliverance from Egypt's tyranny by the hand of Moses; and the many acts that showed the Divine grace and pity, and the Divine fidelity to all the promises He made to His people, and to the hopes He created by His covenant. He hath showed His people the power of His works in giving them the heritage of the heathen. Oliver Cromwell says:—

"What are all our histories but God manifesting Himself, that He hath shaken and tumbled down and trampled upon everything that He hath not planted." The themes and services of the Church are full of memorials of His grace, living witnesses that His mercy endures for ever.

Lives that Make Music.

"Blessed is the man that feareth the Lord."
—PSALM CXII. and vs. 1—10.

1. *The Ideal Life.*

THIS song, like its predecessor and companion, bears beautiful traces of the poet's art, at the same time that it pulses with the fine feelings of the poet's soul. Its impulse, like that of its twin psalm, comes from the singer's passionate desire to behold the glory and splendour of the works of God; but chiefly, in this case, as seen in that unique handiwork of the Eternal, the life, character, and achievements of the Godlike man. For as the former psalm makes music concerning the "works" of God, so these strains are keyed to the honour of a human life fashioned after God's.

That celebrates the praises of Jehovah, glorious in His holy and beneficent activities, fearful in praises, doing wonders. This tells the advantages of those who follow His example, repeat His generosities, achieve His righteousness, and exhibit

> The calm beauty of an ordered life
> Whose every breathing is unworded praise.

Taken together the two psalms tell us that if the flawless and redemptive government of God inspires praise, surely the behaviour of the men He makes like Himself must mirror the Divine thought, stir admiration, and create adoring song. It is the man whose spirit is bathed with the fear of God, and whose heart finds its exultation and rapture in surrender, without reserve, to Him and His method and laws; who meets every morning as a messenger from His presence, and every duty as something that is to be received and gone through, in such a heavenly way as becomes a son of God—it is he who is here the subject of study; it is his justice and mercy and humility, his

Reasonable service of good deeds,
Pure living, tenderness to human needs,
Reverence, and trust, and prayer for
    light to see
The Master's footprints in our daily ways,

that quickens the soul to glad and thankful praise.

An early father said, "The glory of God is a living man, and a living man is the vision of God." But to see that vision in unclouded light we must study man, not at his lowest but at his best; man as he is "conformed to the image of God's Son." "A Christian is the highest style of *man.*" He is renewed in the spirit of his mind, created in righteousness and true holiness; the "workmanship"—or as Paul says "the true poem" of God. To know man, as to know Nature, we must begin at the top—at the perfect flower, not at the buried root. We cannot interpret Nature accurately and fully except in the terms of the richer revelation given us in man; and we cannot understand man save as we study him at that stage of his growth and development in which he is most godlike, that is, most joyously subject to God's authority, and most completely swayed with reverence for His august majesty and greatness.

To the Hebrew the *summum bonum* is the fear of Jehovah. The way of happiness is that of reverence for the Eternal power that made and is making us still, according to the Divine ideal the Father formed of us from the beginning. "The three reverences" of Goethe—for what is above us, and around us, and within us—point to the same goal.

Belief in and reverence for God is the life of man, the beginning of wisdom and work, the end of learning and living, the stay of the soul in sorrow and darkness; the source of patience under the sufferings that torture us by night and by day; the rainbow of hope that proclaims a happy issue out of all our afflictions, the force that makes for justice and truth, for manliness and brotherhood.

Hence the Psalmist finds in the life of a godly man the theme of his praise. Thoreau said, "Every man is a revelation to me"; is it surprising then that man at his best, man made in the likeness of the perfect Son of God, should afford us a vision of God, of His ideas, radiant grace, winning tenderness and triumphant method? Great is the saying of Jesus: "He that hath seen Me hath seen the Father," yet in lower measure and with diminished fulness Paul may say the same of himself in his spiritual regeneration; of his loyalty to his Master; of his self-sacrifice, and of his devotion. As we see men "full of faith and of the Holy Ghost" we call upon our souls and all that is within us to "Praise the Lord."

2. *The Gain of Goodness.*

If the first verse of this psalm describes the qualities of the man of God, the next tells the gains that reach him through his goodness; gains not for himself first and primarily, but for his family and race. It will go well with his house; his children shall rise up to lead the life of the world, and to perpetuate from generation to generation the race of upright, God-fearing, God-obeying men.

The Jew's eye was always on the future. His golden age had to come. It was the far-off Divine event to which the whole creation moved, and it was the distinctive blessing of reverent and right-doing men that their issue gained advantage from the goodness of their progenitors and reaped the harvest they had sown. The Hebrews cared for posterity. A new generation was the hope of the world. It offered oblivion for the prejudices and follies of the past. It gave a fresh start for the future, and foretold a certain, if delayed, success. Not theirs the selfish cry, "after me the deluge," but rather "after me and by me, and because of my trust in God, and obedience to His commandments, there shall be nobler manners, purer laws, deeper faith, braver devotion, fuller service, a real growth in peace and wealth and in goodness."

Godliness is not a bad investment. If the first fruit of the wholly true man is the integrity and saintliness of his children, the second is the increase of his working stock and capital. "Wealth and riches are in his house," and his righteousness stands for ever as a monument to his character. Goodness has a distinct economic value. It pays in the market. It has the "promise of the life that now is"—though the "promise," owing to the industrial conditions and legislative arrangements of modern society, is very often broken. Still, it has the *promise*, because it is the tendency of goodness to make a man careful and thrifty, to develop his business faculty of clear-sightedness, and to stimulate the fullest use of his powers; and so it comes to pass that, in a rightly-ordered society, wealth and riches are in the good man's house, because righteousness is in his heart.

The study of the inheritance of the saints in the work of past ages, and the assured conviction that our little obediences not only train the heart, the will, and the conscience, and discipline our souls for the ministries of heaven, but also lead our children to greater obediences, and stock the world with its best and most enduring wealth, ought to constrain us to praise God for the indefeasible and eternally reproductive issues of good-doing. The growing wealth of the world, due to the growing goodness of men, says: "Praise ye the Lord!"

3. *Light in Darkness.*

But suppose the dark and gloomy day comes, and wealth and riches fail, and our devotion to justice only brings us contumely and scorn, defeat and disgrace, persecution and death! What then? Why this, says the long history of sainthood: "To the upright there ariseth light in the darkness." Written in the biographies of the men of God, from Abel to Abraham, and from Abraham to Moses, and from

Moses to David, and from David to the prophets, is the legend: "The Lord is always mindful of His own," "He keepeth the feet of His saints," "The hand of our God is upon all them for good that seek Him." "The souls of the righteous are in the hands of God, and there shall no torment touch them. In the sight of the unwise they must die; and their departure is taken for misery; and their going from us to be utter destruction; but they are in peace."

"Unto the upright there ariseth light in the darkness." "How far that little candle throws its beams" the singer knew not when he lit it and set it in its candlestick so that it might give light to all that sit in the darkness and shadow of death! What bruised hearts have been healed by its soft radiance! How many a pilgrim has picked his way by its rays, or found grace to stand still and wait uncomplainingly for the further guidance of God! No tongue can tell its history! It would make another Bible, to write out the story of the fortitude and hope, the patience and sweet resignation created by this one line of praise!

I will not linger over so sweet a word, except to point the *moral* seen and stated by the wise man as the result of his own experience. Every star of God shining in the dark sky of our troubled life has written across it in lines of light and beauty the words, "He is gracious and full of compassion, and righteous."

That is what every such event means. That is the Scripture given by the inspiration of God in all such transfiguring experiences; and we fail in our duty unless we read it, mark it, learn it, and inwardly digest it.

"He is gracious" coming to us in His gentleness and lovingkindness. He is full of compassion, of active pity; and He is righteous.

He helps because it is right to help. He heals the broken heart because it is right to heal. He binds up their wounds because it is right. To the impulse of pity there comes the force of righteousness, and therefore He is near to deliver and redeem.

Carry that with you, and you will be at peace. Hallelujah! He doeth all things well.

4. *Securities for Peace.*

The remaining verses describe the godlike soul as not only believing in God and gladly obeying the Divine law, but as believing not less in man as a brother; and exulting in the opportunities life affords for adventurous generosity and kindly ministry, wide and far-reaching beneficence, and the establishment of all life on the eternal foundations of justice. The second table of the law is written on his life and achievements. He loves his neighbour, and shows his love in his actions: he deals graciously with him and "lends" himself out to him for service. He is willing to risk his property in his hands if he may thereby give him a chance of regaining his feet and making his own way: and he risks "hilariously," as Paul puts it, that to which men cling with such pertinacious pluck and fight for with such insatiable greed.

It is a fine portrait of the genuinely godly man of all ages. There is not only a "sweet reasonableness" in his spirit which clothes all he does with beauty and grace; but there is a *splendid venture*, a sort of divine recklessness in his benevolence that puzzles and bewilders Judas and the economists, but wins the approval of the pitiful heart of Christ. He gives, hoping for nothing again. He works without his eye on fee, fame, applause money, or aught else. He simply loves to help, and he does it, commending his love towards men in that, whilst they are not appreciating him, yea, even while they are condemning him, insulting him, he speaks and toils for them. It is a chivalrous generosity that does not spend all the time of the severe frost in collecting statistics and gathering information, and when the genial and kindly spring comes issues a report, and then sinks into the easy-chair of apathy. He shows something of the audacity that Jesus commends when He says, " Give to every one that asks," and if a man takes away your goods, do not ask him for them again. (Luke vi. 31, 38.)

The ninth verse continues the description of the godlike soul: "he has scattered abroad, he has given to the poor: his righteousness abides eternally." He matches the grace of his giving by the width and comprehensiveness of his ministry to the needs of men, and crowns his generosity by his unwavering fidelity to justice. It is in the blending of these qualities that the perfect beauty of the God-renewed nature is seen. The world needs pity, but it needs justice more than pity, and righteousness more than bread. It is the unjust conditions of our social and industrial state that require our thought, and that can only be removed by genuinely religious men.

To such a just and generous soul four rewards are certain: (1) If he gets into a court of justice he maintains his cause, for his character is sound to the core, and his freedom from the sordid and huckstering spirit brings him advantage. (2) He enjoys external security; he stands on the stable rocks of brotherhood and justice. He cannot be moved. (3) Outwardly protected, he is also serene and fearless in temper. Evil tidings do not alarm him; his heart is fixed trusting in the Lord. (4) He attains an honourable name and fame. His horn is exalted. The righteous are held in everlasting remembrance. Hallelujah! Praise ye the Lord!

Strength for Tired Men.

"And the Lord said unto Moses, Is the Lord's hand waxed short? now shalt thou see whether My word shall come to pass unto thee or not."
—Num. xi. 23 (Rev. Ver.).

I.

Moses is tired. Great, strong soul that he is, even he flinches at the sight of the utter breakdown of his work. Meekest, most self-controlled of men, still his long-disciplined spirit comes to the end of its patience, and breaks out in frank unreserve about the uselessness of his service, and in audacious challenge of the wisdom of proceeding with his God-given task. Severe friction has worn the machine so deeply that it threatens to stop; and Moses prays passionately that it may stop, and stop at once!

It is not surprising that the great leader should be weary, fretful, and impatient. Could any work be more exacting than that of conducting a religious war against the priests and princes of Egypt with such an undisciplined horde of soldiers as he had in charge? Already the struggle had issued in the expatriation of a whole race of men, and sent them on their way through a wilderness in search of a new, but still distant, home. To begin such a conflict required prodigious faith and undying courage; and, as we know, Moses shrank from the undertaking with the reluctance of Abraham from killing his son Isaac with his own hand, or of Jeremiah from accepting the perils of the prophet's call—a reluctance which was only finally conquered by the patient entreaty and guaranteed help of God. But to maintain that war, after the first excitements had spent themselves, and to turn the victories he had won over Pharaoh and his priests to advantage, when the irregular and mixed army he had to lead was breaking into rebellion against him, was enough to make the stoutest heart quail, and fill the bravest with despair.

For a moment Moses does quail, and begs to be well rid of his work. He is tired of it—tired to the soul of him. His bold audacity is quenched like the dew by the hot sun, and he looks on the mightiest enterprise of his life as lost beyond all chance of recovery. His gospel is hidden. The splendid exodus is only a tantalising mirage. The god of sensuality sways the "mixed multitude" on the skirts of the pilgrim host, and blinds the eyes of the children of Israel to the Divine ideals, whose beauty had captured their imagination and fired their zeal. Nothing more can be done with such a people.

They are untrained; and the untrained are impatient and petulant, weak and intractable. They move by impulse, collapse at the first touch of trial, and, like the spoilt children of fortune when the toys of the nursery are broken, fret and cry as though the heavens were blotted out. *" And Moses heard the people weeping throughout their families, every man at the door of his tent: . . . and Moses was displeased,"* and forthwith challenged the wisdom that put so heavy a burden upon his shoulders, and impeached the justice that treated him as though he were responsible for the existence and happiness and behaviour of the tumultuous crowds that followed him. "Have I," he exclaimed, "conceived all this people? Have I brought them forth that Thou shouldest say unto me, Carry them in thy bosom, as a nursing-father carrieth the sucking child, unto the land which Thou swarest unto their fathers?"

Indeed, it seems to Moses as though God has failed to keep His contract, ceased from leading His people, refused to check their depraved tastes, to supply their wants, and to share with His servant all the evil, as well as all the good, of His chosen. So with the daring of one who reels and totters from a wholly unexpected blow, he passionately cries out: "O God, if this tragic failure is my fate, kill me out of hand! If Thou hast any love for me, take me away at once! Let me not see my wretchedness! I cannot bear to behold the debrutalising of these half-emancipated men by this 'mixed multitude'! Let me not live, but die!"

It is the fierce outburst of a heart crushed to the point of breaking, and yet in its very despair clinging to the living God!

II.

"Clinging to God," like the ivy to the oak in a violent storm, like a frightened child to its mother when the thunder booms along the sky, like Jacob to the angel at the dawning of the day of his encounter with Esau. Moses will not let God go. His work may be scattered like the clouds before the winds, his hopes may perish as dust; but with desperate energy and unsubduable faith he makes his appeal to the Divine favour, even when it is for the swift and sudden ending of his miserable life. Not for one moment does he dream of taking his future into his own hands. God is his strength, even in his despair, and his expectation is only from Him, when it is the hope and expectation of death. He is in the "depths," but not so deep that he cannot see God and cling to Him, though it be with sorely aching heart, and cry to Him, though it is to cut short his days. He has no other thought, no other refuge from the storm of wretchedness gathering around him with such deafening howl. Therefore, naturally as to his trusted Master he carries his shattered work, fearlessly as to his one just and fair Friend he makes his last appeal, believingly as to One who is unchangeably true and infallibly wise, he pours out all the bitter sorrows of his heart. So the splendid audacity of unconquerable faith in the Eternal breaks through this paroxysm of anguish, and reveals the hidden strength of the greatly daring man. It is a foregleam of that pathetic scene of a later day, when, on the cross of Calvary, the suffering Son of God utters the piercing cry in His bewildering pain and awful loneliness, "*My God, My God*, why hast Thou forsaken Me?" and thus testifies that He endures the cross, as seeing the face and holding the hand of Him who is invisible. There is the fount of power for tired men, the source of peace, the pledge of victory. "In the Lord Jehovah we have everlasting strength." Hold on to Him, O wearied son of man! amid the ghastly ruins of thy faithful toil. Despair not! Take hold on the Eternal, and all shall yet be well. "He shall bring forth thy righteousness as the light, and thy judgment as the noonday." Do not lose heart. The river has only gone underground to appear again. Success is not tested by the outward, but by the inward, not by numbers and content and quiet, but by the sway of ideas and the advance of righteousness. Good work never dies. True-hearted labour for God must be victorious. It is with Him; He loves it and will care for it. Let us not lose Him, and we shall never lose it.

III.

Note, again, it is to God, not to man, Moses goes in his trouble and anger. The people he leads are wayward and weak as children, and as exasperated as their hunger can make them; but he does not complain to them. He remembers they are dust, and betakes himself to the God who made them and gave him his mission for them. His patient labours are frustrated by battalions of "casuals" from the "vagrant populations" of the wilderness; but he does not chide them: he arraigns the Infallible at his tribunal, and carries all his complaint to God.

Hot is his displeasure at the turn of events, and scorching is his wrath; and he does not make the slightest attempt to abate either as he comes into the presence of the Lord. Like Jonah, he feels he does "well to be angry," and, like

Jonah, he cries to the Lord in his affliction out of the belly of hell. He has no disguises or subterfuges; he is great in speech as he is angry in mood; and therefore, with what seems to us inexcusable irreverence, he flings one defiant appeal after another against the Lord and Judge of his life and destiny. His moods change, but not his place: he abides in the court of the Almighty. His impeachment is an act of ineffable courage; but it is also a witness to the intrinsic reality of the man, to the immense strength of his faith in God, and to the completeness of his surrender of himself to Him and to the working out of, or submission to, His sovereign will.

The real tests of character find us out in our tired and angry hours, and reveal our weakness and strength, our mental and spiritual resources, our working interpretation of life and destiny, our unvoiced but deeply ingrained scepticism, or our resolute and world-defying trust in our Father. In our sunnier moods and more vigorous experiences it is not easy to distinguish between the energy due to physical exuberance and ebullience of spirit, and the result of faith and principle, of calculated and habitual steadfastness to conviction. It is when we are under the stress of the storm that blows to the ground the fine edifices that cost us years to build, the reserves of our manhood are called up, and our faith and convictions are under the hottest fire.

Most of us regard our weariness as a licence for grumbling, and the collapse of our work as a warrant for indolence. We interpret failure as a vindication of the fundamental human right to grumble "at large," and we do grumble very much at large. In our saner moments we say it is of little use, though it may add some zest to a monotonous existence and whet a morbidly dull appetite, and we even denounce all dead grumblers, such as the Israelites, for their loquacious discontent; and then, alas! on the first occasion we incontinently repeat their complaints. The tongue is the last member to get tired; and when we can do nothing else, we take the stopper out of the vials of our chronic moroseness and let their vitriolic contents flow freely on friend and neighbour, husband or wife, child or citizen, the Church or the world, instead of keeping our vials for ourselves and going to God with our troubles, and seeking light and strength and rest in Him.

In Bunyan's picture of the pilgrims it is the Hill of Difficulty that shows the difference between Formalist, Hypocrite, and Christian. They travel together till this hill rises before them; then they part. Formalist took one low road called Danger, and was led into a great wood; Hypocrite took another, named Destruction, which led directly to a wide field full of dark mountains, where he stumbled and fell to rise no more; whilst Christian betook himself to the spring of prayer to God, and then went up the hill, saying,

This hill, though high, I covet to ascend;
The difficulty will not me offend;
For I perceive the way to life lies here.
Come, pluck up heart, let's neither faint
 nor fear.
Better, though difficult, the right way
 to go,
Than wrong, though easy, where the end
 is woe.

So Moses goes to the spring of prayer and awaits the Divine decision on his work. Alone he cannot advance; he must fail. Overborne by the tremendous pressure of his task, he tells God he would rather die than be without His guidance. By faith, he who refused to be called the son of Pharaoh's daughter, and asserted his independence of the splendour of courts and the pomp of kings, here clings to God, casts the whole burden of his destiny upon Him, and so escapes the common human malady of wasting his energies in bitter denunciations of his fellows, or in vain regrets over their weaknesses and follies. It was a great faith, and it won a great victory.

IV.

But that victory over himself is only part of the gains secured by communion with God. God listens patiently and soothingly to the indignant hero, and His gracious listening heals his broken heart and binds up his wounds. He hears his complaint out to the very end, without check or rebuke; and then, as if to assure him that his work is not in vain, directs his next steps, supplies him with hints for a "new departure," and assures him of the unbroken continuance of his power. The Divine magnanimity reveals sympathy with his limitations. God's large tolerance for his weakness looks like the recognition of the elements of justice in his complaint, and is thus a sweet solace.

We all know how, when our hearts have been fretted and grieved, the quiet and patient listening of a friend to our story has hushed our agitations and made us at peace; and soon we have seen our work in a new light, and our failures and disasters have worn an altogether different aspect. So Moses sees light in God's light, and learns that "his increase of task" is natural and inevitable. Instead of being a sign of the Divine forgetfulness, it is a witness to His favour and the fulfilment of the promise that He who began the good work will carry it on to perfection. Fidelity is not rewarded with a notice to quit, but by the ascent to a wider field and a larger responsibility. More work to do is the sign of work already well done. It is not the idle and apathetic who are pushed to the front: it is the man who is loyal in "the trivial round, the common task." " Thou hast been faithful over a few things, I will make thee ruler over many things," is the law of the Kingdom of God. "Here," says Matthew Arnold, "is the very sign and condition of each new stage of spiritual progress —*increase of task*. The more we grow, the greater is the task which is set us. This is the law of man's nature and of his spirit's history. The powers we have developed at our old task enable us to attempt a new one; and this again brings with it a new increase of powers."*

That is the deep meaning of this great hour in the full and throbbing life of Christendom: for never did the Divine tasks gather around

* "St. Paul and Protestantism," p. 143.

the world's workers as they do today; never was the service of man so crowded with difficulty, so multiform and so exacting; never were we in greater danger from the surging "mixed multitudes" pressing on and into the better life of the world; and by natural consequence never were there so many victims to spasms of tiredness and despondency. Even the prophets grow weary, and sigh for rest. It is a time of reaction, of national apathy and social fatigue. Like Moses, we fret and chafe at the unprecedented accumulation of responsibilities for the salvation and leadership of the world—responsibilities for the guidance of the ancient races of India and China into the ways of Christ and His gospel; responsibilities for the protection of the lives and liberties, the purity and the homes of the oppressed populations of Europe and Asia; responsibilities for the just government and wise education for self-government of the many subject-peoples and races of Great Britain; responsibility for answering in the terms of Christianity the menacing problems of industry and of social life; and responsibilities for suppressing the beast in men, checking the return to low animal appetites and passions of the masses of our large towns, who welcome pleasing but corrupting literature, and yield in a thousand ways to the debasing power of sin.

And whilst opportunity grows to appalling heights, man himself is beaten back into the brute by those who fatten on his vices and fill their pockets through his excess of riot. Men have " vested interests " in the sufferings and sins of their brothers, and proceed as from securely defended citadels, out of our social and national institutions, to delay the march of their countrymen to the promised land of purity and sobriety, justice and goodness.

Man allies himself with the baser elements in the social and political organism, takes sides with the forces of poverty and ignorance, debauchery and crime, against his fellow. God's Israel is crippled, as of old, by a "mixed multitude."

The voices of a retrograde humanity buzz around and fill the ears of the pilgrims with sounds that stir envy of men and rebellion against the laws of God. And, therefore, it seems to us all the struggle is in vain; all the yearning and planning, the praying and paying, the self-sacrifice and the suffering, issue in failure. We make no perceptible headway, and so we sink into apathy and succumb to old and hoary evils. The Sunday-school teacher forgets and forsakes his class. The temperance crusader retires before the opulent vigour and matchless resource of the omnipotent "trade." The social worker scorns the fine ardours of his youth, and becomes as cold, censorious, and covetous as the men he then denounced. The preacher, faint and weary, sits in his study and asks, "Who hath believed our report? and to whom is the arm of the Lord revealed?" We echo the melancholy of Wordsworth, as he gazed on the ghastlier earlier effects of the French Revolution, and say,

> I lost
> All feeling of conviction, and, in fine,
> Sick, wearied out with contrarieties,
> Yielded up moral questions in despair.
> This was the crisis of that strong disease,
> This the soul's last and lowest ebb; I drooped,
> Deeming our blessèd reason of least use
> Where wanted most.

No, no; let us rather shout, Why art thou cast down, O my soul? Hope thou in God. Tell all to Him! He healeth the broken in heart, and bindeth up their wounds. He soothes us into tranquillity, inspires us with new courage, and prepares us to welcome the old task with new hope and new strength.

> In the secret of His presence
> All the darkness disappears,
> For a Sun that knows no setting
> Throws a rainbow on our tears.
> So the day grows ever lighter,
> Broadening to the perfect noon;
> So the way grows ever brighter,
> Heaven is coming near and soon.

V.

But that is not all. God is light as well as healing. He "fulfils Himself in many ways," and through many persons, "lest one good custom should corrupt the world," or one good man fail in steadfastness and devotion. He discloses to Moses unexpected resources in men to whom He has given the same spirit as to himself, and who are therefore fitted to share in his increase of task. As at the outset of his ministry to Israel, God made up for the deficiency of Moses as a talker by the eloquence of Aaron, so now He completes his equipment for the new demands upon him by the skill and sympathy and the spiritual endowments of the Seventy.

It is God's way. No worker is complete in himself. The best men are but fragments. Moses needs his brother's tongue. Israel's elders will supplement the champion's toil. The seventy disciples go out in pairs. Melancthon is a helpmate to Luther. Zwingli is aided by Leo Judæ. John Wesley finds solace and support in his brother Charles and in the company of preachers. In our weariness God bids us discover inspiration in the fellowship of service, and, by the aid of allies of like temper and aim, add to the efficiency, and increase the success, of our work.

Nor may we be mechanical and arbitrary in our search for comrades or our acceptance of fellowship. Welcome Eldad and Medad as well as the specially designated Seventy; they have the Spirit; and the possession of the Spirit is the permanent and universal quality. "There are diversities of gifts, but the same Spirit." The world is not so poor as we think. We do not know all God's prophets; we do not see the "seventies" waiting to help in the redemption of the world; the Eldads and Medads, who are willing and even eager to carry the burdens that are crushing the life out of us. But they are there, waiting for the hour when we shall discover the folly of our narrow monopolist spirit and the essential unspirituality of our tests of qualification for Divine service.

God is not a pedant. He does not tie Himself down to our rules, and bank up the outflow of His energies within our "orders." He gives His Holy Spirit to them that ask Him! In that which is best, in the supreme possessions of life,

Eldad and Medad are one and equal with the Seventy, and even with Moses himself. They are not drilled in the same way; they are not alike in mental view, in moral achievement; but they are one in the mighty swell of adoring trust, in loyalty to the Divine will, in the force that flushes men with moral impulse and renders them irresistible, in the rhythm and majesty of their march towards righteousness and goodness. Therefore "lift up your eyes on high," O wearied men of God! Gaze into the spiritual order, and "see who hath created these, that bringeth out their host by number: He calleth them all by name; by the greatness of His might, and for that He is strong in power, not one is lacking. Why sayest thou, My way is hid from the Lord, and my judgment is passed away from my God? Hast thou not known? hast thou not heard? the everlasting God, the Lord, the Creator of the ends of the earth, fainteth not, neither is weary; there is no searching of His understanding. He giveth power to the faint; and to him that hath no might He increaseth strength."

"Is the Lord's hand waxed short? now shalt thou see whether My word shall come to pass unto thee or not."

VI.

That "word" does "come to pass." The story ends in tragedy, as it began in rebellion and murmuring. The hand of the Lord is strong to punish; the word of the Lord is a word of doom. Lust and wrong cannot triumph. God is righteous. This is a moral world. If men will reject God, they must know what rejection means. If they will not live according to law they must bear the penalties annexed as sanctions to those laws. *Kibroth-hattaavah*, the graves of lust, show that destruction follows sin.

Intensely as God feels with His suffering people, yet He is so faithful to His character as a just God, that He punishes that He may save, makes men learn by their mistakes, permits them to have what they want till they loathe it, "rather than make them machines that would just go when they are wound up." Times of punished sin are times of progress; and, therefore, deep as is our pity for those who suffer for their conscious evil doings, yet it is some solace to the conscience in us to feel that the life of man is ruled in justice, and that evil does not get off free. "We do not faint," for "we believe" that we shall "see the goodness of the Lord in the land of the living." We are resolute and hold up permanently against the woes of the world, because we are sure that the world somehow constitutes a

Divine order. "The Lord reigneth; let the earth rejoice. The Lord is King among His saints; let them be joyful in Him." He rules in righteousness, and rules out evil. He must win. His counsel stands fast.

> Though we fail indeed,
> You .. I .. a score of such weak workers, He
> Fails never. If He cannot work by us, He will work over us.

It is for us to fight. Say, we are repulsed, and our life's business shows much attempted and nothing achieved; still, let us "stifle the hideous fear that looms out from the dark places of the heart" and say, "Return to thy rest, O my soul; for the Lord hath dealt bountifully with thee." Or, if that is too much for us, let us share the Divine patience, rest in the Divine love and wisdom, and so

> Grow willing, having tried all other ways,
> To try just God's.

The Idea of Eternity in the Bible and Human Life.

THE Scriptures prove themselves in manifold ways to be a Divine echo of the human heart as well as a unique revelation of the will of God. Jehovah often interprets, better than we can ourselves, the thoughts, yearnings, and hopes which sway our souls, and His voice finds a response from the profounder depths of our spiritual nature more readily than any other we are privileged to hear. Not only is this the case with the truths He communicates to us, but even in the mode and degree in which some of those truths enter into the structure of the Bible there is a striking resemblance to, in fact an almost perfect transcript of, the experience of men.

The conception of the immortality of man crops up in the field of inspiration as it does in that of every-day life, now so abruptly as to compel every traveller's gaze, and now so unobtrusively that only practised and sympathetic eyes can discover it. As the idea is not always, perhaps only occasionally, strongly felt by men, so it is not luminously present on every page of Scripture. But as the shadows of eternity are ever falling on the common scenes of daily duty and daily care, so athwart the pages of God's Word there are glimmerings of the light of the unseen world. Doubtless some portions of the book and the life do not immediately betray the presence of the powers of the world to come, but it would be extremely hazardous to declare that their influences are absolutely absent from any page of the former or fragment of the latter. For as men living in the very centres of worldliness, in an atmosphere saturated with time and sense, often catch glimpses of eternity, so there may be seen ensigns and symbols of the invisible world in the biographies of Haman and Mordecai, the scepticism of Ecclesiastes, and the whirlwind of doubts that rushes through the book of Job. The imperious instinct of immortality, which persists in asserting that our individual existence is not closed when the curtain falls on the stage of our earthly activity, urged the Hebrew long ages since to a similar anticipation in the wilderness, gave him a joyful song in Zion's temple, and an unfailing solace by the waters of Babylon. Natural religion has always intimated a coming day of retribution. The children of a "locust-eaten past" have ever looked forward to the rich harvest of an all-compensating future. The logic of the conscience has generally conducted men to the belief in a time when the discords of sin will be hushed in the harmonious music of a regenerated world. Suffering and wronged man has learned to project his being into another and rectifying state, and in his dying hours has been sustained by a vivid faith in brighter and never-ending scenes. The descendants of Abraham enjoyed all the results of such a training, and possessed in addition the special revelation of God.

Hence on the pages of Hebrew literature man is seen fervently desiring the eternal. His soul thirsts for the living, the ever-living God. Oppressed with a sense of weakness and weariness, vexed with the vanity of life's intensest struggles, and threatened with the speedy and irresistible approach of death, he seeks a refuge that can never be invaded, a home that outlives all generations, and a portion that continues to satisfy when heart and flesh shall have failed for ever. Everywhere the Old Testament reveals the immortal God. He is the same, and His years change not. His being abides unaffected amid exhaustless vicissitude. He is the Lord Jehovah in whom there is everlasting strength. His counsel stands fast for ever and ever, and the thoughts of His heart to all generations. His laws know no change. Made with an infinite foresight, they embrace the necessary adaptations to all the varieties of human circumstance, and the exigencies of different ages and climes. On the solid rock of His eternal truth men anchor in safety and are never moved. On His infinite purity they confidingly gaze, for its glory can never be dimmed. From His power they constantly draw, for it is as inexhaustible as it is gentle and tender. In the midst of His mercies they dwell, full of peace and hope, giving thanks with a glad heart because His mercy endureth for ever. The God of the Hebrew is always the Eternal and Almighty Leader of His people.

But the idea of God's eternity generates in the atmosphere of inspiration, and as by a natural law the conception of man's illimitable future. Because He lives we shall live also, is an axiom to the Christian consciousness. The notion, not the fact, of our enduring existence springs in a nature like ours out of the knowledge of His immortality. There is a heaven for us because there is a God, and we have a personal subjective eternity of being because there is a personal, real, and eternal Deity. The roots of all life are in God, and man soon learns to see his own immortality clearly when he has seen God's. The book, therefore, that discovers to us the "I am that I am," will scarcely be barren concerning the future of men.

Nor is it. The creation of Adam in the Divine image is the audible whisper of this fundamental fact of man's spiritual nature, and though the first sin defaces, it does not completely efface the stamp of eternity impressed on his brow. The victory of Abel's faith was not eclipsed by his cruel death, but forthwith proclaimed by pæans of angels in a cloudless land. Enoch walked with God and was not. But why? Because death had seized him with relentless grasp? Because the grave held him with tightening grip? No: God took him to be with Himself. Abram, cheered by promise, eagerly looked for a city whose foundations were firmer than Zion's, and whose builder was God. Job, cast down, but not destroyed, bravely battled with hosts of objections, taunts, and insinuations, marshalled by his friends, and victoriously sung of his faith in the Everlasting Redeemer who could not fail him in the latter day. Moses, reared in the lap of Egyptian plenty, dowered with the riches of Egyptian learning, flushed with the bright hopes of an Egyptian crown, boldly casts all aside, preferring the care and society of the people of God because he has respect, not to the pleasures of sin, which are but for a season, but to the recompense of an enduring reward. Elijah ascends to heaven, not as a death-vanquished captive, but as a living victor in a fire-chariot of triumph. David drew abundant comfort from the well of expectation, and sung at once of his Lord's ascent from the grave, and his own satisfaction in conscious resemblance to God after death. Daniel taught the captive Jews that "the wise shall shine as the brightness of the firmament, and they that turn many to righteousness as the stars for ever." The fact still lives in the book of Wisdom. Jesus met with it amongst the current conceptions of His day, brought it to the light of His life and illuminated it, carried it to its stable throne by His resurrection; and since then it has ruled almost without intermission the faith of the Christian Church, and given an unprecedented dignity and value to man all over the world.

To say, then, that this fundamental fact of man's spiritual nature is not taught in the Old Testament is to commit two mistakes. It confounds, in the most glaring way, the definitions of a creed with the declarations of truth, and dogmatic representation of a belief with its existence in and dominion over the soul. It forgets that truths which powerfully affect the springs of human action, colouring thought, controlling emotion, and directing will, often fail to put themselves obtrusively forward in the noisy talk of the senate, the market, and the street. Read the more ancient Scripture in the light of every-day experience, and it will be seen that as Nature nowhere formulates her laws, but incessantly obeys them, moving along with an almost unbroken quiet, so the revelations of God and man in Scripture are all cast in the mould of the idea of eternity.

The Better Resurrection.

"The better resurrection."—HEBREWS XI. 35

In a letter dealing expressly with the "better things" of Christianity as compared with Judaism, it was to be expected that the "resurrection" would have a place. For "our Saviour Christ Jesus has abolished death and brought life and incorruption to light through the gospel." The promise by which He allured men to trust in His love was, "He that heareth My word, and believeth Him that sent Me, hath eternal life, and cometh not into judgment, but hath passed out of death into life." To Martha, sorrowing concerning her dead brother, Christ spoke the good news. "I am the resurrection and the life: he that believeth in Me, though he die, yet shall he live: and whosoever liveth and believeth on Me shall never die." He "who died for our sins was raised for our justification."

Therefore nothing so stirred the faith, or fed the courage, of the first disciples of the Lord as the assurance of immortality. They "preached Jesus and the resurrection." They defied death and the grave through Him who was the death of death, the defeat of sin, and the beatification of martyrdom. "O death, where is thy sting?" was the boastful challenge they flung at the "Shadow feared of man"; "O grave, where is thy victory?" the defiant taunt with which they looked into the grave's bottomless depths. They exulted in the "better resurrection."

But what is the "better resurrection"? When does it occur, and what are its attendant circumstances and consequences? "Better" is a word of comparison.

What is the resurrection with which it is contrasted, and on which it is an improvement?

All the contrasts of this Epistle are between the old religion and the new; the things that accompanied the history and experiences of the ancient Hebrew, and the things of which the saints of the new covenant were the possessors and heirs; hence this comparison is between the two outstanding "resurrections" of the Old Testament annals, and the "resurrection" of Christ and of the Christian, foreloomed to the faith and hope of the great heroes of Maccabean story. "Women," says the writer in his swift and stirring recital of the luminous conquests of a faith that ventured all for God, "women received their dead by resurrection; and others were tortured, not accepting deliverance, that they might obtain *the better resurrection.*"

Clearly his imagination is fired

by those two pathetic incidents of domestic life in which the prophets Elijah and Elisha exhibit the splendour of their trust in the Eternal God, and receive their reward in the rescue of two children from the grip of death. He sees the widow of Sarepta, cowed by superstitious fear, reading the arrival of the prophet as a menace to her home, hears her plaintive cry as though her worst fears were justified, when her beloved son falls sick and dies, and then watches with joy the undisturbed seer take the dead boy and pray to God, till the soul of the child comes into him again and he revives. Nor could he forget the way in which Elisha repeated the heroism of his leader, when "the great woman of Shunem," who had welcomed the prophet to the hospitality of her home, fell into sore trouble through the loss of her one child, went to him in her sorrow, and he healed her breaking heart by the restoration of her beloved boy, the one solace of her widowed heart. So the harps broken by the fingers of death were retuned by the faith of the seer, and the families that had been clouded in gloom and oppressed with loss were again buoyant with the fulness and strength of young life.*

That is one picture, but it suggests another and another. Great were those events, but they were signs of greater. Poets and seers were Elijah and Elisha, for they dwelt in God and with God; but they were left far behind in the race of faith and courage by "others" like Isaiah† and Eleazar, ‡ and the heroic mother and her seven sons,§ who were tortured, broken on the wheel, refusing to accept

---

* 1 Kings xvii. 17; 2 Kings iv. 18.
† Tortured by Manasseh, according to the account in "The Ascension of Isaiah."
‡ 2 Maccabees vi. 18, 31.
§ 2 Maccabees vii.

the deliverance offered to them at the cost of their loyalty to the cause of their country and to God, so that they might obtain "the better resurrection," and ascend to the life that is without fault or sin, and where there is fulness of joy and pleasure for evermore.

Therefore "the better resurrection" is the resurrection of the New Testament rather than that of the Old; but not the resurrection of the daughter of Jairus, or of the son of the widow of Nain, or of the brother of Martha and Mary, but of Jesus Christ and of all who believe in Him; the resurrection proclaimed by Peter and the rest of the Apostles, and of which Paul spoke as though it were the goal of all his striving and the sum of all his hopes.

The first resurrection was good, for it was a return to the light of the sun, to the love of the home, and to the work of life; but the second was *better*, for it was the advent of the spirit to the light that is never clouded, to the love that knows no sorrow, and to the work that never wearies or exhausts. The first was to corporeity and the resumption of the duties and pleasures of earth, but the second was better, for it was to the life of the spirit in its fulness and perfection. That was the renewal of a lease on property of incomputable value, but of a lease that, however long it is, is still short. This was the entrance into the house not made with hands, eternal in the heavens. That was a restoration to experiences that in their widest sweep are restricted, and in their loftiest ascents yet fall short of the eternal; but this is admission into the Father's house, with its infinite roominess and its endless stages of discovery and of growth from age to age. The son of the Shunem widow may have died again even in its childhood;

the children of Jairus and of the widow of Nain were carried to the grave a second time. Lazarus was buried again. Dorcas had to leave the poor she loved and for whom she toiled, though at a later date; but Isaiah and Eleazar escaped to the life everlasting, and to the joys of the perfect home of the saints of God.

William Blake, the painter-poet, as he lay dying, said, "He was going to that country he had all his life wished to see," and just before he died " he burst into singing of the things he saw." The seer saw "the better resurrection," the glorious ascent to the larger and purer life of the coming world, and rejoiced in the sight. By all that heaven is better than earth, the second "resurrection" is better than the first; and therefore Charles Kingsley scarcely need have prayed as he faced death, "God forgive me! but I look forward to it with an intense and reverent curiosity." Without at all disparaging the life that now is, and finding in it as we ought an ever-growing joy, yet God means us to look forward to the further and freer stages of our spiritual development with keen interest and holy joy.

Again, the return to the streets of Shunem and of Nain of the youths that had gone through the gates of death was the resumption of the educational and disciplinary experiences of the present life; and since these are of God, they too are good; but the "resurrection" of Isaiah and Eleazar was to a life of progress freed from the inevitable "imperfections," the necessary and inevitable limitations that bound our life, right and left, and hinder us in all directions. We go where the vision is no longer blurred and dimmed, where perceptions are clear, judgments accurate, and conclusions safe. We dwell where the horizons are no longer low and narrow, but entrancingly high and vast. We soar out of the reach of the perplexities of the "flesh," the struggle with temptation, the pain of self-sacrifice, the agony of sin, and dwell where we see all things in God, where we utterly and perfectly love God, and, in sacrificing ourselves to God, rest wholly in Him. John Howe had no more welcome thought of heaven than its freedom from sin. To rise to that! Oh, think of it, battling son of God; what joy unspeakable and full of glory. To continue the life of love and of aspiration, of joy and of service, under *such conditions;* and to find again what we have lost—of holy purpose, of struggling faith, of fervent desire —this is indeed the " better resurrection."

> There shall never be one lost good!
> What was, shall live as before;
> The evil is null, is nought, is silence
> implying sound;

What was good shall be good, with, for
    evil, so much good more;
  On the earth the broken arcs; in the
    heaven a perfect round.

All we have willed or hoped or dreamed
    of good shall exist;
  Not its semblance, but itself; no
    beauty, nor good, nor power
Whose voice has gone forth, but each
    survives for the melodist
  When eternity affirms the conception
    of an hour.

The high that proved too high, the heroic
    for earth too hard,
  The passion that left the ground to
    lose itself in the sky,
Are music sent up to God by the lover
    and the bard;
  Enough that He heard it once: we shall
    hear it by-and-by.

But the writer to the imperilled Hebrew Christians is not writing a thesis on the soul's immortality, or citing a witness to the reality of the life after death. His purpose is practical. He is feeding faith, clearing the sight of the soul, nourishing patience, and firing courage. A better faith is created by the expectation of the "better resurrection." The "women" easily believed in the power of God's prophet to kill and to make alive. Accept the doctrine of an Almighty God, and faith in the resurrection is easy; but it required insight and patience, and a venture on God of immense force, to refuse to escape from being burnt over a slow fire in the anticipation that when the body was burnt to a cinder the *man* would be alive with God. It is a finer spirit which bears pain and loss, and the scorn and despisal of men, for the sake of truth and goodness and duty, in the confident assurance that the next life will righten this, than is that which merely sings in church, "I believe in the resurrection of the body." It is a far greater achievement to be ready to die like Luther or Paul, in the conviction that right and truth and God claim loyalty to conscience, and that the Eternal takes into His keeping those who witness for Him, than it is to affirm adherence to all the creeds of all the churches. It was that faith that was in Paul when, clad in the gladiator's garb, he fought with beasts at Ephesus; and it is the same faith in the things unseen and eternal, in the invisible Father and Saviour, that must be in us, if at the soul of us we are to be absolutely real, intrinsically sincere.

Let then the "better resurrection" solace you for the lives whose sun went down while it was yet day—the careers that began in fine promise and have gone out in darkness. They have not *arrived here;* but they are for ever with the Lord, and they will arrive.

Bring immortality into your life. Take long views. Infancy prepares for childhood, childhood for youth, youth for manhood, and all for eternity. Plan your life on that scale; the "things unseen" are the real things. Fight for faith in the "better resurrection." Struggle to keep it strong. It is precious beyond estimate. Do not let it slip from you; you are the children of the Eternal. Trust the Risen and Ruling Redeemer. Because He lives, you shall live also.

LONDON:
W. SPEAIGHT AND SONS, PRINTERS,
FETTER LANE.

www.ingramcontent.com/pod-product-compliance
Lightning Source LLC
Chambersburg PA
CBHW030315170426
43202CB00009B/1015